CHRIS DEVON

Full-Stack Development with Node.js

First edition

This book was professionally typeset on Reedsy.
Find out more at reedsy.com

Contents

Introduction

In a world where web and application development is continually evolving, becoming a skilled full-stack developer with Node.js can open doors to dynamic opportunities. This book is designed to serve as a complete guide, helping you acquire the knowledge and hands-on experience to build robust, scalable applications using Node.js. Here's how to approach this journey to maximize your learning experience.

Purpose of the Book: Building a Job-Ready Full-Stack Developer Skillset

As a full-stack developer, you need both breadth and depth in various aspects of web development—working on both the client and server sides, managing data flow, implementing secure and efficient code, and deploying scalable applications. This book has been structured to equip you with practical skills, project-based experience, and deep insights into how modern full-stack development works, particularly using the Node.js ecosystem. By the time you finish, you should be confident in your ability to:

- Build, test, and deploy a variety of applications, from simple to complex.
- Collaborate effectively with other developers using established workflows.
- Understand industry-standard tools and techniques, from DevOps to database management.

How to Use This Book: Project-Based Learning Approach

This book takes a hands-on approach, which means each chapter goes beyond theory to give you an actionable, project-focused learning path. You'll be creating projects that mirror real-world applications—such as a blogging platform, e-commerce sites, and secure RESTful APIs. Every project is designed to build on the previous one, giving you a progressive learning experience that reinforces each new concept while adding another layer of complexity.

Each chapter includes:

- **Practical Projects**: Tackle full-stack projects that develop both backend and frontend skills, deepening your understanding of each layer in the stack.
- **Key Concepts and Examples**: Learn the "why" and "how" of each technology, exploring not just how to use a tool or framework but understanding its underlying architecture.
- **Challenges and Self-Assessment**: Reflective challenges after each chapter ensure that you can apply what you've learned and independently tackle problems.

This approach is well-suited for self-taught learners, coding bootcamp graduates, and developers familiar with other stacks who want to transition into Node.js.

Overview of Key Tools and Technologies

Full-stack development requires familiarity with various tools. Below is a quick look at some of the core technologies we'll be using throughout the book:

1. **Node.js**: At the core of the backend, Node.js is an open-source, cross-platform runtime that enables JavaScript to be used server-side. Fast, powerful, and efficient, Node.js is ideal for building scalable applications.
2. **Express**: As the web framework for Node.js, Express provides a lightweight and flexible approach to building web servers and APIs. It's well-suited for creating RESTful services and middleware layers.
3. **React/Vue.js**: These frontend libraries are designed to create dynamic, user-friendly interfaces. We'll focus on the basics of integrating frontend frameworks with Node.js to create a seamless full-stack experience.

4. **MongoDB & SQL Databases**: We'll cover both SQL and NoSQL databases, as each has distinct use cases in web development. MongoDB, a NoSQL database, is a natural fit for handling dynamic data, while SQL databases like MySQL offer structured data handling with powerful querying capabilities.

5. **DevOps Tools (Docker, CI/CD, Cloud Deployment)**: Today's developers are expected to understand the basics of deployment and DevOps. We'll cover these topics to ensure your projects are ready for real-world application environments.

Suggested Learning Path for Beginners, Intermediate, and Advanced Developers

This book is designed to accommodate various skill levels. Beginners will find that each chapter builds incrementally, allowing them to focus on core fundamentals. Intermediate developers will benefit from advanced sections, which dive deeper into topics like security, performance optimization, and deployment. Advanced readers can use the book as a reference guide, especially in sections that explore microservices architecture and DevOps.

Here's a suggested approach based on your experience level:

- **Beginners**: Start from Chapter 1 and follow each section sequentially. Take your time with foundational concepts to ensure a strong understanding of full-stack fundamentals.
- **Intermediate Developers**: If you're comfortable with the basics of JavaScript and web development, you can focus on more complex chapters like data optimization and microservices.
- **Advanced Developers**: Use this book as a practical reference, dipping into specific chapters for insight on DevOps practices, scalability, and advanced optimization techniques.

Your Full-Stack Journey Starts Here

This book is not just about code; it's about mastering the techniques and practices that will make you an effective full-stack developer. With each chapter, you'll gain not only technical skills but also the confidence to build complex applications from scratch, deploying them and maintaining them in real-world environments.

Ready to embark on this journey? Let's dive in and start building.

Getting Started with Full-Stack
Development and Node.js

W hat is Full-Stack Development?
To build a complete web application, two primary components
are essential: the frontend and the backend. Full-stack
developers manage both, ensuring that the frontend and backend work
harmoniously together.

1. **Frontend (Client-Side)**: This is what the user sees and interacts with.
   Typically built using HTML, CSS, and JavaScript, the frontend focuses
   on creating a smooth user experience. Frameworks like React and Vue.js
   are popular choices for handling user interfaces and building dynamic
   content.
2. **Backend (Server-Side)**: The backend processes data, handles business
   logic, and connects the frontend with a database. It's responsible for
   responding to frontend requests, running complex computations, and
   ensuring that data flows securely and efficiently. In full-stack Node.js
   development, Express.js is the most commonly used framework for
   creating a fast, scalable backend.

As a full-stack developer, you'll learn to handle both these components, creating applications where the frontend and backend communicate seamlessly.

Why Node.js for Full-Stack Development?

Node.js is built on Chrome's V8 JavaScript engine and allows developers to run JavaScript code server-side. This is advantageous for full-stack development because:

- **Single Language for Client and Server**: JavaScript can be used across both the frontend and backend, making development more efficient and consistent.
- **High Performance**: Node.js handles many concurrent connections with ease, thanks to its non-blocking, event-driven architecture.
- **Vibrant Ecosystem**: The Node Package Manager (npm) provides access to countless libraries and tools that streamline development, allowing you to focus on building rather than reinventing.
- **Scalability**: Node.js excels at handling real-time applications and is ideal for applications that require continuous connections, such as chat platforms and streaming services.

By mastering Node.js, you position yourself to build fast, scalable, and maintainable applications.

Setting Up Your Development Environment

To start building applications, we'll first need to set up a few essential tools:

- **Installing Node.js and npm**
- Download and install Node.js from the official website (https://nodejs.org). Ensure you select the LTS (Long Term Support) version, which is more stable for development.
- Node.js comes bundled with npm (Node Package Manager), which we'll use to manage libraries and dependencies.
- **Installing Visual Studio Code**
- Visual Studio Code (VS Code) is a powerful, free code editor that's widely used for JavaScript development. Download and install VS Code (https://code.visualstudio.com).
- Set up key extensions, like ESLint for code quality, Prettier for formatting,

and GitHub Copilot (optional) for AI-driven coding assistance.
- **Setting Up Git for Version Control**
- Git is essential for tracking changes in your projects, especially when working collaboratively or managing multiple versions. Download and install Git (https://git-scm.com).
- Create a GitHub account if you don't have one, and configure Git to link with your account.
- Learn basic Git commands: git init, git add, git commit, git push, and git pull.

Project: Building Your First "Hello World" Server

Let's start by creating a simple "Hello World" server to get comfortable with Node.js and Express.

- **Initialize a New Node.js Project**
- Create a new directory for the project. Open your terminal and run:

```
mkdir hello-world-server
cd hello-world-server
```

- Initialize a new Node.js project with npm:

```
npm init -y
```

- This creates a package.json file, which will manage your project's dependencies.
- **Installing Express**
- Express is a lightweight framework that makes it easy to create servers with Node.js. Install it by running:

```
npm install express
```

- **Creating the Server**
- In your project directory, create a new file called app.js. Open app.js and add the following code:

```
const express = require('express');
const app = express();
const PORT = 3000;

app.get('/', (req, res) => {
  res.send('Hello World!');
});

app.listen(PORT, () => {
  console.log(`Server is running on http://localhost:${PORT}`);
});
```

- **Running the Server**
- Start the server by running:

```
node app.js
```

- Open your browser and navigate to http://localhost:3000. You should see "Hello World!" displayed, indicating that your server is running successfully.
- **Understanding the Code**
- The above code creates an Express application that listens on port 3000. When you access the root URL (/), it sends a "Hello World!" response.

8

This simple project demonstrates the basics of using Node.js and Express to create a web server. From here, we'll expand on this foundation, building more complex applications.

Git and GitHub for Version Control: Basics and Best Practices

Version control is essential in modern development. It allows you to keep track of changes, collaborate with others, and manage different versions of your code. Here's a quick introduction to using Git with GitHub:

- **Setting Up a Repository**
- In your project directory, initialize a new Git repository:

```
git init
```

- Stage your changes and commit them:

```
git add .
git commit -m "Initial commit"
```

- **Pushing to GitHub**
- Go to GitHub and create a new repository.
- Link your local repository to GitHub:

```
git remote add origin <repository-url>
git push -u origin main
```

- **Best Practices**

- Commit frequently, with clear, concise messages.
- Use branches for new features or experiments, merging into the main branch only after testing.
- Collaborate by pushing changes and creating pull requests, a key work-flow for team projects.

Core Concepts of Node.js and Asynchronous Programming

U nderstanding the Node.js Architecture: V8 Engine and Event Loop At the heart of Node.js is the **V8 JavaScript engine**, developed by Google for Chrome. V8 compiles JavaScript directly into machine code, enabling faster execution. But Node.js adds something unique to the mix: the **Event Loop**.

- **The V8 Engine**:
- V8 is a high-performance JavaScript engine written in C++. It compiles JavaScript code to optimized machine code before execution, enabling JavaScript to run extremely fast.
- When Node.js is built on V8, it inherits this speed and performance, making it possible to use JavaScript on the server side.
- **The Event Loop**:
- Node.js operates on a **single-threaded** model, but it can handle thousands of requests simultaneously, thanks to its non-blocking, asynchronous design.
- The **event loop** is the mechanism that enables this. It acts as a manager, continuously checking for tasks, executing them, and offloading operations like I/O to the system, so it doesn't block the main thread.
- When an I/O operation, like reading a file or making a network request, is called, Node.js hands it over to the system and moves on to the next task. Once the I/O operation completes, it returns to the event loop for

further processing.

Synchronous vs. Asynchronous Programming

In synchronous programming, tasks are executed in sequence, with each operation waiting for the previous one to complete. This can lead to bottlenecks, especially with time-consuming operations like database queries. Asynchronous programming, however, allows other tasks to proceed while waiting for long-running operations to complete, improving efficiency and responsiveness.

- **Synchronous Programming Example**:

```
const fs = require('fs');

const data = fs.readFileSync('file.txt', 'utf8'); // Blocks until file is read
console.log(data);
console.log('File has been read!');
```

- In this synchronous example, the program will wait for fs.readFileSync to complete before moving to the next line. This blocking behavior can lead to delays, especially if file.txt is large.
- **Asynchronous Programming Example**:

```
const fs = require('fs');

fs.readFile('file.txt', 'utf8', (err, data) => {
  if (err) throw err;
  console.log(data);
});
console.log('File reading initiated!');
```

- Here, fs.readFile is non-blocking, meaning the program initiates the read operation and immediately moves to the next line. The callback function will handle the result when the file is ready, allowing other tasks to proceed without delay.

Callbacks, Promises, and Async/Await: Key Asynchronous Patterns

Asynchronous programming in Node.js typically uses one of three main approaches: **callbacks**, **promises**, and **async/await**. Understanding these is essential to writing effective, readable asynchronous code.

- **Callbacks**:
- In the early days of Node.js, callbacks were the primary method of handling asynchronous tasks. However, callbacks can lead to a messy structure known as **callback hell**, where callbacks are nested within each other, making the code hard to read and maintain.
- Example of a callback:

```
const fs = require('fs');

fs.readFile('file.txt', 'utf8', (err, data) => {
  if (err) return console.error(err);
  console.log(data);
});
```

- **Promises**:
- Promises provide a cleaner syntax for handling asynchronous operations and allow chaining. A promise represents a future value that can either be **resolved** (operation successful) or **rejected** (operation failed).
- Example of a promise:

```
const fs = require('fs').promises;

fs.readFile('file.txt', 'utf8')
  .then(data => console.log(data))
  .catch(err => console.error(err));
```

- **Async/Await**:
- Introduced in ES2017, async/await allows asynchronous code to be written in a synchronous style. An async function returns a promise, and the await keyword pauses the function execution until the promise is resolved or rejected.
- Example of async/await:

```
const fs = require('fs').promises;

async function readFile() {
  try {
    const data = await fs.readFile('file.txt', 'utf8');
    console.log(data);
  } catch (err) {
    console.error(err);
  }
}

readFile();
```

- This structure makes asynchronous code easier to read and avoids the nested structure of callback hell.

Error Handling in Node.js: Best Practices for Robust Code

Error handling is critical in asynchronous code. Errors can be thrown by unexpected failures, such as failed API calls or file access issues. To handle errors gracefully, we can use **try/catch** blocks, especially with async/await, and carefully chain .catch() methods with promises.

- **Callback Error Handling**:
- Always pass an error as the first argument in a callback. This allows you to handle any issues within the callback function.
- Example:

```
const fs = require('fs');

fs.readFile('file.txt', 'utf8', (err, data) => {
  if (err) {
    console.error('Error reading file:', err);
    return;
  }
  console.log(data);
});
```

- **Error Handling with Promises**:
- Use .catch() to handle errors in promises.
- Example:

```
const fs = require('fs').promises;

fs.readFile('file.txt', 'utf8')
  .then(data => console.log(data))
  .catch(err => console.error('Error reading file:', err));
```

- **Error Handling with Async/Await**:
- Use try/catch blocks around await statements to catch errors.
- Example:

```
async function readFile() {
  try {
    const data = await fs.readFile('file.txt', 'utf8');
    console.log(data);
  } catch (err) {
    console.error('Error reading file:', err);
  }
}
```

Project: Building an Asynchronous Data Fetcher with Node.js

Let's create a simple project that demonstrates the power of asynchronous programming by fetching data from an external API. This project will show how to use async/await with error handling to make HTTP requests.

- **Setup**:
- Initialize a new Node.js project and install axios, a popular library for making HTTP requests:

```
mkdir async-data-fetcher
cd async-data-fetcher
npm init -y
npm install axios
```

- **Creating the Data Fetcher**:
- In app.js, create an asynchronous function that fetches data from a public API and logs the result.

```
const axios = require('axios');

async function fetchData() {
  try {
```

```
    const response = await
    axios.get('https://jsonplaceholder.typicode.com/posts');
    console.log(response.data);
  } catch (error) {
    console.error('Error fetching data:', error);
  }
}

fetchData();
```

- Run this code with node app.js, and observe the console output. You should see the fetched data or an error message if the request fails.
- **Understanding the Code**:
- Here, axios.get is an asynchronous function that returns a promise. By using await, we pause the execution of fetchData until the promise resolves.
- The try/catch block handles any errors that may occur during the fetch operation, ensuring that our application doesn't crash if an error arises.

Building RESTful APIs with Node.js and Express

Introduction to RESTful Architecture

REST (Representational State Transfer) is an architectural style for designing networked applications. RESTful APIs use HTTP requests to perform operations such as GET, POST, PUT, and DELETE on data resources. The key principles of RESTful design include:

1. **Statelessness**: Each request from a client must contain all the information the server needs to fulfill that request. The server does not retain any client-specific data between requests, making the API more scalable.
2. **Client-Server Separation**: The client and server should interact only through the API, with no dependency on each other's internal implementation.
3. **Uniform Interface**: REST APIs use a standardized URL structure and HTTP methods to interact with resources, making them easy to understand and consume.
4. **Resource-Based URLs**: Each resource (such as users, posts, or products) should have a unique URL, such as /api/users or /api/products. This makes the API intuitive and logical.

Understanding these principles is critical to creating well-designed APIs that are easy to use, extend, and scale.

Setting Up Express for API Development

To start building RESTful APIs, we'll use **Express**, a fast and minimalist framework that simplifies the process of creating HTTP servers in Node.js. Let's set up a new project and install the necessary dependencies.

- **Initialize a New Project**:
- Create a new directory for your API project and navigate into it:

```
mkdir restful-api
cd restful-api
```

- Initialize the project with npm:

```
npm init -y
```

- **Install Express**:
- Install Express along with nodemon (a utility that automatically restarts the server when changes are made):

```
npm install express
npm install --save-dev nodemon
```

- **Configure the Project**:
- In the package.json file, add a script to start the server with nodemon:

```
"scripts": {
  "start": "nodemon index.js"
}
```

- **Create the Server**:
- Create an index.js file, which will be the entry point for our API. In this file, we'll set up a basic Express server:

```
const express = require('express');
const app = express();
const PORT = process.env.PORT || 3000;

app.use(express.json());

app.listen(PORT, () => {
  console.log(`Server running on http://localhost:${PORT}`);
});
```

- This setup prepares the server to listen for incoming requests on a specified port, with JSON support enabled.

Designing REST Endpoints: GET, POST, PUT, DELETE

In this section, we'll define endpoints for common HTTP methods used in REST APIs. To illustrate these concepts, let's build a basic API for managing a collection of books.

- **Define the Data Structure**:
- Create a simple array to store book data temporarily. In a production API, this would be replaced with a database.

```
let books = [
  { id: 1, title: '1984', author: 'George Orwell' },
  { id: 2, title: 'To Kill a Mockingbird', author: 'Harper Lee' },
];
```

- **GET Requests**:
- A GET request retrieves data from the server. Let's create two endpoints: one to get all books and another to get a specific book by ID.

```
// Get all books
app.get('/api/books', (req, res) => {
  res.json(books);
});

// Get a book by ID
app.get('/api/books/:id', (req, res) => {
  const book = books.find(b => b.id === parseInt(req.params.id));
  if (!book) return res.status(404).send('Book not found');
  res.json(book);
});
```

- **POST Requests**:
- A POST request creates a new resource on the server. We'll create an endpoint to add a new book to our collection.

```
app.post('/api/books', (req, res) => {
  const newBook = {
    id: books.length + 1,
    title: req.body.title,
    author: req.body.author,
  };
```

```
  books.push(newBook);
  res.status(201).json(newBook);
});
```

- Note: The req.body property holds the new book data, so ensure express.json() is set up to parse JSON requests.
- **PUT Requests**:
- A PUT request updates an existing resource. We'll create an endpoint to update a book's title and author.

```
app.put('/api/books/:id', (req, res) => {
  const book = books.find(b => b.id === parseInt(req.params.id));
  if (!book) return res.status(404).send('Book not found');

  book.title = req.body.title;
  book.author = req.body.author;
  res.json(book);
});
```

- **DELETE Requests**:
- A DELETE request removes a resource from the server. We'll create an endpoint to delete a book by ID.

```
app.delete('/api/books/:id', (req, res) => {
  const bookIndex = books.findIndex(b => b.id ===
  parseInt(req.params.id));
  if (bookIndex === -1) return res.status(404).send('Book not
  found');

  const deletedBook = books.splice(bookIndex, 1);
```

```
  res.json(deletedBook);
});
```

With these endpoints, our API supports CRUD (Create, Read, Update, Delete) operations, covering the basic functionality of any RESTful API.

Using Postman for Testing APIs

Before deploying, it's essential to test your API thoroughly. **Postman** is a popular tool for testing APIs, allowing you to simulate requests, inspect responses, and debug issues.

- **Install Postman**: Download Postman from https://www.postman.com and install it.
- **Testing GET Requests**:
- Open Postman and create a new GET request to http://localhost:3000/api/books.
- Send the request and check that it returns a list of books.
- Repeat this for other endpoints, using path variables (e.g., /api/books/1 for a specific book).
- **Testing POST, PUT, and DELETE**:
- **POST**: Set the method to POST and add JSON data in the body:

```
{
  "title": "The Catcher in the Rye",
  "author": "J.D. Salinger"
}
```

- **PUT**: Send a PUT request to http://localhost:3000/api/books/1, updating the book's title and author.
- **DELETE**: Send a DELETE request to http://localhost:3000/api/books/1 and verify the book is removed.

Postman enables you to test and confirm that your API functions as expected across all endpoints.

Implementing Basic CRUD Operations with Express

With our CRUD operations established, let's look at some best practices to improve our API:

- **Validation**:
- Ensure that incoming data is validated before adding it to the database. This prevents issues caused by malformed or incomplete data. For example:

```
app.post('/api/books', (req, res) => {
  if (!req.body.title || !req.body.author) {
    return res.status(400).send('Title and author are required');
  }
  const newBook = { /*...*/ };
});
```

- **Response Codes**:
- Use appropriate HTTP response codes to indicate the result of each request. For instance, 201 Created for successful POST requests, 400 Bad Request for validation errors, and 404 Not Found for nonexistent resources.
- **Error Handling**:
- Implement centralized error handling middleware to manage errors uniformly, improving code readability and reliability.
- **Middleware for Reusability**:
- Break down common functionalities, like logging requests or validating data, into middleware functions for modular, reusable code.

Project: Creating a RESTful API for a Blogging Platform

Now, let's apply what we've learned by creating a RESTful API for a basic blogging platform.

- **Define Endpoints**:
- We'll build endpoints to handle operations on blog posts, including creating, reading, updating, and deleting posts.
- **Set Up Data Structure**:
- Use an array or a database (like MongoDB) to store post data.
- **Implement Authentication (Optional)**:
- Add basic authentication to secure API routes for creating, updating, and deleting posts.

Database Essentials – Working with SQL and NoSQL

SQL vs. NoSQL: Choosing the Right Database for Your Project
Before we dive into the technicalities, it's important to understand the fundamental differences between SQL and NoSQL databases:

- **SQL (Relational Databases)**:
- SQL databases store data in **tables**, with relationships between tables defined by **foreign keys**.
- SQL databases follow a **structured schema**, making them ideal for applications with well-defined data models.
- Common SQL databases include **MySQL**, **PostgreSQL**, and **SQLite**.
- SQL databases are generally ACID-compliant, meaning they ensure data consistency through **Atomicity**, **Consistency**, **Isolation**, and **Durability**.
- **NoSQL (Non-Relational Databases)**:
- NoSQL databases store data in a variety of structures, including **documents**, **key-value pairs**, **graphs**, and **wide-column stores**.
- They provide more flexibility, as they are **schema-less** and can handle unstructured data more efficiently.
- Common NoSQL databases include **MongoDB** (document-based), **Redis** (key-value store), and **Cassandra** (wide-column).
- NoSQL databases excel at **horizontal scaling** and can handle massive amounts of data across distributed systems.

In summary, SQL databases are suited for structured data with complex relationships, while NoSQL databases are better for handling large, flexible datasets without a predefined schema.

Introduction to MongoDB (NoSQL) and MySQL (SQL)

To cover the essentials of both types, we'll focus on **MongoDB** as an example of a NoSQL database and **MySQL** as an example of an SQL database.

- **MongoDB**:
- MongoDB is a document-oriented database where data is stored in **JSON-like documents** with a flexible schema. It's highly scalable and is often the database of choice for modern applications that handle large volumes of unstructured data.
- **MySQL**:
- MySQL is a widely-used relational database that stores data in tables. It's structured, powerful, and highly suitable for applications with defined data models. MySQL supports complex queries, joins, and transactions, which are essential for applications requiring data integrity.

Connecting Node.js with MongoDB Using Mongoose

Mongoose is a popular ODM (Object Data Modeling) library for MongoDB, which simplifies data modeling and interaction with MongoDB. Here's how to set up Mongoose and integrate it into a Node.js application.

- **Installing MongoDB and Mongoose**:
- First, ensure MongoDB is installed and running on your machine. You can download it from https://www.mongodb.com/try/download/community.
- In your Node.js project, install Mongoose:

```
npm install mongoose
```

- **Setting Up a MongoDB Connection**:
- In your project, create a db.js file to handle the database connection:

```
const mongoose = require('mongoose');

mongoose.connect('mongodb://localhost:27017/mydatabase', {
  useNewUrlParser: true,
  useUnifiedTopology: true
})
.then(() => console.log('MongoDB connected'))
.catch(err => console.error('MongoDB connection error:', err));
```

- Replace 'mydatabase' with the name of your database. Ensure MongoDB is running locally or replace localhost:27017 with the URI of your MongoDB server if using a hosted solution.
- **Defining a Schema and Model with Mongoose**:
- With MongoDB's flexible schema, you can define a model that enforces a structure for your documents. Create a schema and model for a basic user collection:

```
const mongoose = require('mongoose');

const userSchema = new mongoose.Schema({
  name: String,
  email: { type: String, unique: true },
  age: Number
});

const User = mongoose.model('User', userSchema);

module.exports = User;
```

- Here, we create a User model that represents the collection in MongoDB.

28

This model will allow us to perform CRUD operations on the users collection.

- **CRUD Operations with Mongoose**:
- **Create a Document**:

```
const newUser = new User({ name: 'John Doe', email:
'john@example.com', age: 30 });
newUser.save()
  .then(user => console.log('User created:', user))
  .catch(err => console.error('Error creating user:', err));
```

- **Read Documents**:

```
User.find()
  .then(users => console.log('Users:', users))
  .catch(err => console.error('Error finding users:', err));
```

- **Update a Document**:

```
User.findOneAndUpdate({ email: 'john@example.com' }, { age: 31 },
{ new: true })
  .then(user => console.log('User updated:', user))
  .catch(err => console.error('Error updating user:', err));
```

- **Delete a Document**:

```
User.findOneAndDelete({ email: 'john@example.com' })
  .then(user => console.log('User deleted:', user))
  .catch(err => console.error('Error deleting user:', err));
```

Mongoose simplifies database interactions, allowing you to focus on your application's business logic rather than database intricacies.

Setting Up Sequelize for SQL Database Management with MySQL
  For SQL databases, **Sequelize** is an ORM (Object-Relational Mapper) that makes it easier to work with MySQL in Node.js, handling SQL queries and data manipulation.

- **Installing MySQL and Sequelize**:
- Install MySQL on your machine and create a new database.
- In your Node.js project, install Sequelize and the MySQL2 driver:

```
npm install sequelize mysql2
```

- **Setting Up a Sequelize Connection**:
- Create a db.js file and configure the Sequelize instance:

```
const { Sequelize } = require('sequelize');

const sequelize = new Sequelize('database_name', 'username',
'password', {
  host: 'localhost',
  dialect: 'mysql'
});

sequelize.authenticate()
  .then(() => console.log('MySQL connected'))
```

```
.catch(err => console.error('MySQL connection error:', err));

module.exports = sequelize;
```

- **Defining Models and Relationships in Sequelize**:
- Similar to Mongoose, Sequelize allows you to define models that represent tables. Here's how to define a User model:

```
const { DataTypes } = require('sequelize');
const sequelize = require('./db');

const User = sequelize.define('User', {
  name: {
    type: DataTypes.STRING,
    allowNull: false
  },
  email: {
    type: DataTypes.STRING,
    allowNull: false,
    unique: true
  },
  age: {
    type: DataTypes.INTEGER,
    allowNull: false
  }
});

module.exports = User;
```

- With Sequelize, you can define data types, constraints, and relationships such as one-to-many and many-to-many, making it easy to represent complex data relationships.
- **Performing CRUD Operations with Sequelize**:
- **Create a Record**:

```
User.create({ name: 'Jane Doe', email: 'jane@example.com', age: 25
})
  .then(user => console.log('User created:', user))
  .catch(err => console.error('Error creating user:', err));
```

- **Read Records**:

```
User.findAll()
  .then(users => console.log('Users:', users))
  .catch(err => console.error('Error finding users:', err));
```

- **Update a Record**:

```
User.update({ age: 26 }, { where: { email: 'jane@example.com' } })
  .then(() => console.log('User updated'))
  .catch(err => console.error('Error updating user:', err));
```

- **Delete a Record**:

```
User.destroy({ where: { email: 'jane@example.com' } })
  .then(() => console.log('User deleted'))
  .catch(err => console.error('Error deleting user:', err));
```

Sequelize handles database communication through an ORM layer, giving you the ability to work with SQL databases using JavaScript objects and methods.

Project: Building a User Management System with MongoDB and MySQL

To solidify your understanding, let's build a user management system that leverages both MongoDB (for flexible data storage) and MySQL (for structured data).

- **Define User Models for MongoDB and MySQL**:
- Implement a user model in both databases, as demonstrated above, to handle different data scenarios.
- **Implement Routes for CRUD Operations**:
- Create routes to handle user creation, retrieval, updating, and deletion, using Express middleware to handle each operation in the respective database.
- **Integrate Database Logic with Express**:
- Set up routes and controller logic in your Express app to connect with MongoDB through Mongoose or MySQL through Sequelize.
- **Testing and Validation**:
- Test each endpoint with Postman to verify correct behavior and handle errors using middleware.

Advanced Data Management and Optimization Techniques

D
ata Normalization and Denormalization
Data normalization and denormalization are crucial concepts in database design, particularly in SQL databases, where they play an essential role in maintaining data integrity and optimizing storage.

- **Normalization**:
- **Purpose**: Normalization organizes data to minimize redundancy and dependency. This process breaks down large tables into smaller, related tables.
- **Benefits**: By normalizing data, you reduce data redundancy, which minimizes storage costs and makes data easier to maintain and update.
- **Forms of Normalization**:
- **1NF (First Normal Form)**: Ensures that each table cell contains a single value and each record is unique.
- **2NF (Second Normal Form)**: Builds on 1NF by ensuring that all non-key attributes are fully dependent on the primary key.
- **3NF (Third Normal Form)**: Requires that all attributes are only dependent on the primary key, eliminating transitive dependency.
- **Example**:

```
Users Table (Unnormalized)
| ID | Name       | City        | Zip     | State |
|----|------------|-------------|---------|-------|
| 1  | John Doe   | New York    | 10001   | NY    |
| 2  | Jane Smith | Los Angeles | 90001   | CA    |


After Normalization:

Users Table
| ID | Name       |
|----|------------|
| 1  | John Doe   |
| 2  | Jane Smith |


Addresses Table
| UserID | City        | Zip     | State |
|--------|-------------|---------|-------|
| 1      | New York    | 10001   | NY    |
| 2      | Los Angeles | 90001   | CA    |
```

- **Denormalization**:
- **Purpose**: Denormalization combines related tables to reduce the need for complex joins, thereby improving read performance.
- **Benefits**: It's particularly beneficial in read-heavy applications or systems where performance is prioritized over storage efficiency.
- **Example**:
- In a denormalized structure, we could store all user details in a single table rather than separate tables for user details and addresses, as shown in the example above.

Choosing between normalization and denormalization depends on the specific requirements of your application. High read performance applications (e.g., reporting systems) may benefit from denormalization, while transactional applications (e.g., e-commerce platforms) are often normalized for data integrity.

Indexing and Query Optimization for SQL and NoSQL Databases

Indexing is one of the most powerful ways to optimize query performance. It allows databases to locate specific rows much faster, especially in large datasets. However, indexing also increases storage requirements, so it's important to use it strategically.

- **Indexing in SQL Databases**:
- **Primary Indexes**: Automatically created on primary key columns, providing a unique identifier for each row.
- **Secondary Indexes**: Created on columns that are frequently queried. For example, if you often search for users by email, indexing this column can improve search speed.
- **Composite Indexes**: Built on multiple columns, which is helpful when queries filter by more than one column.
- **Example**:

```
CREATE INDEX idx_email ON Users (email);
```

- **Indexing in NoSQL Databases (e.g., MongoDB)**:
- MongoDB allows indexing on fields within documents, including fields in embedded documents and arrays.
- Indexes in MongoDB are highly flexible, allowing you to create **single-field** indexes, **compound** indexes, or even **multikey** indexes for arrays.
- **Example**:

```
db.users.createIndex({ email: 1 });
```

- **Query Optimization**:
- **EXPLAIN Plans**: Both SQL and NoSQL databases offer tools to analyze

queries. For instance, EXPLAIN in SQL or explain() in MongoDB provides insights into query execution.

- **Avoiding Full Table Scans**: Queries that scan entire tables are inefficient. Use indexes and limit the data returned to reduce resource consumption.
- **Optimization Techniques**:
- Use **LIMIT** to restrict the number of rows returned.
- Retrieve only the fields you need rather than all fields.
- Structure your WHERE clause carefully, avoiding unnecessary conditions.

Efficient indexing and query optimization are vital to maintaining high-performance databases, especially as the volume of data grows.

Caching Strategies for Faster Database Access

Caching is an effective way to reduce the load on your database and improve the response time for frequently accessed data. By temporarily storing data in memory, your application can retrieve information faster, bypassing the database for commonly requested data.

- **In-Memory Caching with Redis**:
- Redis is a popular in-memory data structure store that supports caching for various data types (e.g., strings, hashes, lists).
- Use Cases: Cache API responses, session data, or frequently accessed database queries.
- Setting Up a Redis Cache:
- Install Redis locally or use a hosted Redis service.
- Connect to Redis in your Node.js application using the redis package:

```
const redis = require('redis');
const client = redis.createClient();

client.set('key', 'value', redis.print);
```

```
client.get('key', (err, reply) => console.log(reply));
```

- Cache Expiration: Set expiration times on cache entries to ensure they don't become outdated.
- **Database Query Caching**:
- Many databases support built-in query caching. When a query is frequently executed with the same parameters, the database can store the result and retrieve it from memory instead of re-executing the query.
- **Example**: MySQL query cache or MongoDB's in-memory engine.
- **Application-Level Caching**:
- Use application-level caching for dynamic content that changes frequently. For example, caching user data on login, which can reduce the need for repeated queries within a session.

Caching reduces latency and improves user experience, particularly in high-traffic applications or APIs that handle a large volume of requests.

Managing Relational Data with SQL Joins and NoSQL Aggregation
   When working with complex data, you'll often need to combine data from multiple tables or collections. Here's how SQL joins and MongoDB's aggregation framework allow you to do this efficiently.

- **SQL Joins**:
- Joins are used to combine data from two or more tables based on related columns. Types of joins include:
- INNER JOIN: Returns records that have matching values in both tables.
- LEFT JOIN: Returns all records from the left table, with matching records from the right.
- RIGHT JOIN: Opposite of LEFT JOIN, returning all records from the right.
- FULL JOIN: Returns records when there's a match in one of the tables.
- **Example**:

```sql
SELECT users.name, orders.amount
FROM users
INNER JOIN orders ON users.id = orders.user_id;
```

- **MongoDB Aggregation Framework**:
- MongoDB's aggregation framework allows you to perform complex data transformations and aggregations, similar to SQL joins but within a document-oriented structure.
- Pipeline Stages:
- **$match**: Filters documents based on conditions.
- **$group**: Groups documents by specified fields and applies aggregate functions.
- **$lookup**: Performs a left outer join to another collection.
- **Example**:

```
db.users.aggregate([
  { $lookup: {
      from: "orders",
      localField: "_id",
      foreignField: "user_id",
      as: "user_orders"
    }
  },
  { $match: { "user_orders.amount": { $gt: 100 } } }
]);
```

Effectively managing relational data across different database types enables you to query and retrieve complex information efficiently, allowing your application to serve more dynamic and relational data.

Project: Enhancing API Performance with Database Optimizations

Let's apply these advanced techniques in a practical project that optimizes an existing API for an e-commerce application.

- **Create Optimized Database Schemas**:
- Design separate tables/collections for products, users, and orders, applying normalization and denormalization where appropriate.
- **Implement Indexes and Caching**:
- Index frequently queried fields such as product category and user ID.
- Use Redis to cache popular product listings or user sessions.
- **Optimize Complex Queries**:
- Use joins and aggregation frameworks to retrieve data for reporting, such as top-selling products or user purchase history.
- **Monitor and Test**:
- Monitor query performance using database tools (e.g., MySQL's EXPLAIN or MongoDB's profiler).
- Benchmark the API performance before and after applying these optimizations to measure improvement.

Frontend Integration – Building Interactive UIs with React or Vue.js

I ntroduction to Frontend-Backend Communication

Before diving into React and Vue.js, it's essential to understand how the frontend communicates with the backend. In a typical full-stack application, the frontend makes requests to the backend API to fetch or send data. This communication generally happens through **HTTP requests** using libraries like fetch or axios. The backend, in turn, responds with the requested data, which the frontend displays dynamically.

- **RESTful APIs**:
- A RESTful API is the most common way for frontends and backends to communicate in web applications. The frontend sends GET, POST, PUT, or DELETE requests to the backend's API endpoints, and the backend responds with data in JSON format.
- **Frontend Libraries**:
- **Axios**: A promise-based HTTP client that simplifies making API requests in JavaScript.
- **Fetch API**: A built-in JavaScript API for making HTTP requests, suitable for smaller applications or quick API calls.

By connecting the frontend and backend through HTTP requests, you enable the two to work in harmony, providing a seamless experience for end-users.

Setting Up a Basic React Application

React, developed by Facebook, is a powerful JavaScript library for building user interfaces. It allows developers to create reusable UI components, manage state efficiently, and build complex applications with a reactive, component-based approach.

- **Installing React**:
- To create a new React project, use **Create React App**, a CLI tool that sets up a fully configured React application:

```
npx create-react-app my-app
cd my-app
```

- **Basic Project Structure**:
- The Create React App CLI generates the following basic structure:
- **src/index.js**: The entry point for the application, where React renders the root component.
- **src/App.js**: The main component, where you'll build your application's UI.
- **Component-Based Structure**:
- React applications are built using **components**, reusable building blocks that represent different parts of the UI. Here's a simple example:

```
function App() {
  return (
    <div>
      <h1>Hello, World!</h1>
    </div>
  );
}
```

```
export default App;
```

React's declarative nature allows you to focus on how the UI should look based on the application's state, rather than manipulating the DOM manually.

Setting Up a Basic Vue.js Application

Vue.js, developed by Evan You, is another popular JavaScript framework known for its flexibility and ease of use. Vue's syntax is clean and approachable, making it an excellent choice for developers looking to integrate a frontend quickly.

- **Installing Vue**:
- You can create a new Vue project using Vue CLI, which provides a standardized setup for Vue applications:

```
npm install -g @vue/cli
vue create my-vue-app
cd my-vue-app
```

- **Basic Project Structure**:
- Vue CLI generates the following structure:
- **src/main.js**: The entry point where Vue creates and mounts the root instance.
- **src/App.vue**: The main component, where you'll add application logic and UI elements.
- **Single File Components**:
- Vue uses **single file components** (SFCs) with a .vue extension, combining HTML, JavaScript, and CSS into one file. Here's a simple example:

```
<template>
  <div>
    <h1>Hello, World!</h1>
  </div>
</template>

<script>
export default {
  name: "App"
};
</script>

<style>
h1 {
  color: #42b983;
}
</style>
```

Vue's simplicity and flexibility make it a strong alternative to React for frontend integration.

Fetching Data from Node.js APIs: Axios and Fetch
  Whether you're using React or Vue, the process of fetching data from the backend is similar. We'll use **Axios** in this example, as it's compatible with both frameworks and simplifies handling HTTP requests.

- **Installing Axios**:
- Add Axios to your React or Vue project:

```
npm install axios
```

- **Fetching Data in React**:
- In React, you can use the useEffect hook to fetch data when the component loads:

```
import React, { useEffect, useState } from 'react';
import axios from 'axios';

function App() {
  const [data, setData] = useState([]);

  useEffect(() => {
    axios.get('http://localhost:3000/api/data')
      .then(response => setData(response.data))
      .catch(error => console.error('Error fetching data:',
      error));
  }, []);

  return (
    <div>
      <h1>Data from Backend</h1>
      <ul>
        {data.map(item => (
          <li key={item.id}>{item.name}</li>
        ))}
      </ul>
    </div>
  );
}

export default App;
```

- **Fetching Data in Vue**:
- In Vue, you can fetch data inside the created lifecycle hook:

```
<template>
  <div>
    <h1>Data from Backend</h1>
    <ul>
      <li v-for="item in data" :key="item.id">{{ item.name }}</li>
```

```
      </ul>
    </div>
  </template>

  <script>
  import axios from 'axios';

  export default {
    data() {
      return {
        data: []
      };
    },
    created() {
      axios.get('http://localhost:3000/api/data')
        .then(response => this.data = response.data)
        .catch(error => console.error('Error fetching data:',
        error));
    }
  };
  </script>
```

In both frameworks, this code retrieves data from the backend, allowing you to display it on the frontend in real time.

Building Components and Managing State

- **Components in React and Vue**:
- **React**: React uses functions or classes to create components. Each component can maintain its own state using hooks like useState.
- **Vue**: Vue's SFCs combine template, script, and style sections in one file, making components self-contained and easy to manage.
- **Managing State**:
- In React, **useState** and **useReducer** hooks are commonly used to manage local component state. For larger applications, **context API** or libraries like **Redux** handle global state.
- In Vue, **data** properties and **computed** properties manage state locally,

while **Vuex** serves as a centralized store for larger applications.

Project: Integrating a Real-Time Chat Feature in a Node.js App

To showcase frontend-backend integration, let's build a basic real-time chat feature using React/Vue with Socket.IO.

- **Backend Setup**:
- Install socket.io in your backend and create a simple server for chat messages:

```
npm install socket.io
```

- **Frontend Integration**:
- Install socket.io-client in your React/Vue app and create a chat component that connects to the backend.
- **Real-Time Message Display**:
- Display messages in real time, handling incoming messages from the backend.

This hands-on project demonstrates how to integrate a real-time component with a Node.js backend.

Authentication and Authorization

U nderstanding Authentication and Authorization
Let's break down these two essential concepts:

- **Authentication** confirms that users are who they say they are. It's the process that users go through to log in, often requiring a username and password or other credentials like biometric data.
  - **Authorization** determines what an authenticated user is allowed to do within the application. For instance, some users might have access to administrative functions, while others only see general content. Authorization often involves assigning roles or permissions to each user.

Together, these measures protect the application's data and ensure that sensitive areas or functions aren't accessible to unauthorized users.

Implementing JSON Web Tokens (JWT) for Authentication

JWTs are a popular method for managing authentication because they're stateless, meaning the server doesn't need to store sessions for each logged-in user. Here's how JWT works in a typical application flow:

1. **User Login**: The user submits their credentials (e.g., username and password).
2. **Token Issuance**: If credentials are correct, the server generates a JWT containing the user's information (usually in a secure, minimal form)

and sends it back to the client.

3. **Token Storage**: The client stores the token (often in local storage or cookies).

4. **Accessing Protected Resources**: For every request to a protected endpoint, the client sends the token in the request headers, allowing the server to verify the user's identity.

JWTs have three parts: Header, Payload, and Signature. The payload can contain various information about the user, such as their ID, roles, and permissions, but remember to keep this data minimal and avoid sensitive details (like passwords).

Building a Login System with JWT in Node.js

Let's walk through creating a basic login system that uses JWT for authentication.

Step 1: Setting Up the Project

- First, create a new Node.js project with Express and install the necessary dependencies:

```
mkdir auth-system
cd auth-system
npm init -y
npm install express bcryptjs jsonwebtoken dotenv
```

- **File Structure**: Organize the files as follows:

```
auth-system/ ├───────
  .env ├───────
  app.js ├──────
```

```
controllers/  |   └────────
   authController.js  ├──────────
models/  |   └─────────
   user.js  ├────────
routes/  |   └─────────
   authRoutes.js  └──────────
config/  └─────────
   db.js
```

Step 2: Environment Configuration

Store sensitive information in a .env file for security. Add the JWT secret and database credentials:

```
JWT_SECRET=your_jwt_secret
JWT_EXPIRATION=3600
```

Step 3: User Model and Password Encryption

Define a User model with Mongoose, and use bcrypt to hash passwords before storing them. Bcrypt is a hashing library designed specifically for secure password storage.

- **Password Hashing**: Hashing turns the password into a fixed-length, irreversible format. For extra security, bcrypt adds "salt," which is random data added to each password before hashing to make each hash unique.

In models/user.js:

```
const mongoose = require('mongoose');
const bcrypt = require('bcryptjs');

const userSchema = new mongoose.Schema({
    username: { type: String, required: true, unique: true },
    password: { type: String, required: true },
```

```
    role: { type: String, enum: ['user', 'admin'], default: 'user'
    }
});


userSchema.pre('save', async function (next) {
    if (this.isModified('password')) {
        this.password = await bcrypt.hash(this.password, 10);
    }
    next();
});


module.exports = mongoose.model('User', userSchema);
```

Step 4: AuthController and JWT Creation

Set up authController.js to handle registration, login, and token generation.
In controllers/authController.js:

```
const jwt = require('jsonwebtoken');
const bcrypt = require('bcryptjs');
const User = require('../models/user');
const { JWT_SECRET, JWT_EXPIRATION } = process.env;

const register = async (req, res) => {
    // Registration logic
};

const login = async (req, res) => {
    const { username, password } = req.body;
    const user = await User.findOne({ username });

    if (user && (await bcrypt.compare(password, user.password))) {
        const token = jwt.sign({ userId: user._id, role: user.role
        }, JWT_SECRET, { expiresIn: JWT_EXPIRATION });
        res.json({ token });
    } else {
        res.status(401).json({ message: 'Invalid credentials' });
    }
};
```

```
module.exports = { register, login };
```

Role-Based Access Control (RBAC)

In a system with multiple roles (e.g., user, admin), RBAC helps define what each role can access. For example, regular users might only be able to access their profile, while admins can manage other users.

Middleware for Role Checking

To restrict access based on roles, create middleware that verifies the user's role:

In middleware/authMiddleware.js:

```
const jwt = require('jsonwebtoken');
const { JWT_SECRET } = process.env;

const authMiddleware = (roles = []) => {
    return (req, res, next) => {
        const token = req.header('Authorization').replace('Bearer
        ', '');
        if (!token) return res.status(401).send('Access denied.');

        try {
            const decoded = jwt.verify(token, JWT_SECRET);
            req.user = decoded;
            if (roles.length && !roles.includes(req.user.role)) {
                return res.status(403).send('Permission denied.');
            }
            next();
        } catch (error) {
            res.status(401).send('Invalid token.');
        }
    };
};

module.exports = authMiddleware;
```

Use this middleware in routes to protect resources. For example, add the authMiddleware(['admin']) function to an admin-only route.

Managing Sessions and Cookies in Node.js

While JWTs are typically used for token-based authentication, session-based authentication remains common. In session-based authentication, the server stores user session data, and cookies help manage the session's lifetime.

1. **Session Management**: Use Express-session to handle sessions, storing session data on the server and associating it with a cookie on the client.
2. **Cookies**: Cookies hold session data on the client-side, allowing the server to recognize returning users without needing credentials each time.

Project: Creating a Secure Login System with JWT and RBAC

For this project, build a basic login system that restricts routes based on user roles, ensuring only authorized users can access certain parts of the application.

Steps:

1. **Setup Routes**: Define routes in routes/authRoutes.js for registration, login, and protected resources.
2. **Implement Middleware**: Use the authMiddleware to enforce access restrictions on specific routes.
3. **Testing**: Verify that:

- Only authenticated users can access protected endpoints.
- Users with specific roles (like "admin") can access certain routes while regular users cannot.

4. Error Handling:

- Set up informative error messages to guide users through any access issues.

Security Essentials for Full-Stack Development

O verview of Security Threats
Web applications face various security threats that can compromise data integrity, expose user information, and even disrupt business operations. Understanding these threats is the first step toward protecting your applications. Below are some of the most common security risks:

- **Cross-Site Scripting (XSS)**: This occurs when attackers inject malicious scripts into web pages viewed by other users. XSS allows attackers to steal cookies, session tokens, or other sensitive data.
- **SQL Injection**: Attackers use malicious SQL queries to manipulate a database, often leading to unauthorized data access, data deletion, or data alteration. This is particularly relevant in applications that use SQL-based databases.
- **Cross-Site Request Forgery (CSRF)**: CSRF attacks trick users into performing actions they didn't intend, such as transferring funds or changing settings, by exploiting their logged-in state.
- **Man-in-the-Middle (MITM)**: This attack occurs when an attacker intercepts communication between two parties (e.g., a user and server), potentially leading to data theft or alteration.

Being aware of these threats helps you build applications that can effectively prevent them.

Environment Variables and Configuration Management

Environment variables allow you to store sensitive information, such as API keys and database credentials, outside of your codebase. Keeping such data out of your code prevents it from being exposed in version control or inadvertently shared.

- **Setup Environment Variables**: Create a .env file in the root of your project and add your sensitive data:

```
DB_PASSWORD=my_secure_password
JWT_SECRET=your_jwt_secret
```

- **Accessing Environment Variables in Node.js**: Use the dotenv package to load environment variables into your application:

```
require('dotenv').config();
const dbPassword = process.env.DB_PASSWORD;
const jwtSecret = process.env.JWT_SECRET;
```

By securing sensitive configuration data with environment variables, you reduce the risk of accidental exposure.

Using Helmet and Security Middlewares in Express

Helmet is a middleware for Express that helps secure applications by setting various HTTP headers. It's simple to use and provides protection against several common attacks, including XSS and clickjacking.

- **Installing and Using Helmet**:

```
npm install helmet
```

- **Enabling Helmet in Your App**:

```
const helmet = require('helmet');
const express = require('express');
const app = express();

app.use(helmet());
```

Helmet's default settings add multiple layers of security. However, you can also customize its behavior based on your application's needs, like configuring Content Security Policy for added control over the resources your app can load.

Encrypting Data: Hashing Passwords with bcrypt

Storing plain-text passwords is one of the biggest security risks in web applications. Password hashing transforms user passwords into a secure format before storing them, making them extremely difficult to decipher if the database is compromised.

Password Hashing with bcrypt: bcrypt is a powerful library for hashing passwords with salt, which means random data is added to each password before hashing to make each result unique, even if users have similar passwords.

- **Installing bcrypt**:

```
npm install bcryptjs
```

- **Hashing Passwords**:

```
const bcrypt = require('bcryptjs');

async function hashPassword(password) {
    const salt = await bcrypt.genSalt(10);
    const hashedPassword = await bcrypt.hash(password, salt);
    return hashedPassword;
}
```

- **Comparing Passwords**:

```
async function comparePasswords(inputPassword, hashedPassword) {
    return await bcrypt.compare(inputPassword, hashedPassword);
}
```

Hashing passwords adds a strong layer of protection, reducing the likelihood that an attacker can retrieve user passwords in the event of a data breach.

Preventing Cross-Site Scripting (XSS)

XSS attacks occur when attackers inject malicious scripts into web pages, compromising user data and security. To prevent XSS, it's essential to sanitize user inputs and use security libraries.

- **Sanitizing User Input**: Always sanitize and validate user input to remove potentially harmful scripts. Use a library like express-validator:

```
npm install express-validator
```

- **Example of Input Validation**:

```
const { body } = require('express-validator');

app.post('/comment', [
    body('content').isString().trim().escape()
], (req, res) => {
    // Handle the comment submission
});
```

- **Escaping Output in the Frontend**: Ensure that any user-generated content displayed in the frontend is properly escaped. If you're using a templating engine or frontend framework, it should have built-in ways to escape potentially dangerous content.

Avoiding SQL Injection

SQL injection occurs when an attacker injects SQL code into a query, potentially giving them access to the database. This is common with poorly handled user inputs in SQL queries.

Parameterized Queries: Parameterized queries prevent SQL injection by separating SQL code from data inputs. For example, in Sequelize (a popular ORM for Node.js):

```
const { QueryTypes } = require('sequelize');

async function getUserById(userId) {
    const user = await sequelize.query(
        'SELECT * FROM users WHERE id = :userId',
        {
            replacements: { userId },
            type: QueryTypes.SELECT
        }
    );
```

```
    return user;
}
```

By using parameterized queries, you avoid placing raw user input directly in SQL queries, safeguarding your application against SQL injection attacks.

Implementing CSRF Protection

CSRF attacks occur when a user is tricked into performing actions they didn't intend, often by exploiting their logged-in state. You can prevent CSRF by using anti-CSRF tokens, which verify that actions come from legitimate sources.

- **Adding CSRF Protection with csurf**:

```
npm install csurf
```

- **Enabling csurf Middleware**:

```
const csrf = require('csurf');

app.use(csrf({ cookie: true }));

app.get('/form', (req, res) => {
    res.render('form', { csrfToken: req.csrfToken() });
});
```

Using CSRF tokens ensures that only genuine user interactions trigger changes in the application.

Project: Securing an E-commerce API with Security Best Practices

In this project, we'll secure a basic e-commerce API by implementing the security practices we've covered. Here's how to go about it:

Steps:

- **Set Up Basic JWT Authentication**:
- Ensure users are authenticated before accessing sensitive routes like order management or account details.
- **Secure Passwords**:
- Hash all user passwords with bcrypt, preventing plain-text storage.
- **Sanitize User Inputs**:
- Use express-validator to sanitize and validate inputs for all routes that accept user input, such as product reviews and profile updates.
- **Implement Helmet and CSRF Protection**:
- Add Helmet middleware to secure HTTP headers, and csurf for anti-CSRF tokens.
- **Verify Authorization with Role-Based Access**:
- For sensitive routes, confirm the user's role and restrict access accordingly (e.g., only admins can add or remove products).
- **Error Handling**:
- Gracefully handle unauthorized access and provide clear feedback, so users understand what went wrong.

Following these steps will protect your e-commerce API against common security threats, ensuring a safer experience for users and keeping sensitive data private.

Testing and Debugging in Node.js

I ntroduction to Testing: Importance and Types of Tests
Testing is essential to catch issues early and to verify that new features or updates don't unintentionally break existing functionality. Effective testing saves time, reduces bugs, and builds confidence in the application's stability. Let's break down the three main types of tests:

- **Unit Testing**: Tests individual functions or methods in isolation. These tests are the foundation of the testing process, verifying that each part of the code works as expected.
- **Integration Testing**: Verifies that different modules or services work together. This is particularly useful for functions that depend on each other, such as an API interacting with a database.
- **End-to-End (E2E) Testing**: Simulates user actions to test the entire flow of an application. These tests ensure that an application performs as expected from a user's perspective.

Each type of test plays a distinct role in the development cycle, and together they create a comprehensive testing strategy that minimizes issues in production.

Setting Up a Testing Environment in Node.js

To start testing in Node.js, you'll need a testing framework. Popular choices include **Mocha**, **Jest**, and **Chai**. In this chapter, we'll use Mocha for unit testing and Jest for integration and end-to-end testing. Here's how to set up these tools:

- **Install Mocha and Chai**:

```
npm install mocha chai --save-dev
```

- **Install Jest**:

```
npm install jest --save-dev
```

- **Configure Mocha and Jest**: Create scripts in your package.json file for easy test execution.

```
"scripts": {
    "test": "mocha",
    "test:jest": "jest"
}
```

With these frameworks installed, you're ready to start writing and running tests in your Node.js application.

Unit Testing with Mocha and Chai

Unit testing is about verifying that individual pieces of code function correctly. Mocha provides a test framework, while Chai offers assertion functions to define expected outcomes.

- **Basic Unit Test Structure**: A Mocha test typically has describe blocks to organize tests and it blocks for each specific test case.

```
const { expect } = require('chai');
const myFunction = require('../path/to/module');

describe('myFunction', () => {
    it('should return the expected output when called with
    specific arguments', () => {
        const result = myFunction(inputData);
        expect(result).to.equal(expectedOutput);
    });
});
```

- **Testing Asynchronous Code**: When testing asynchronous functions, you can use done in Mocha to wait for the function to complete, or return a Promise.

```
it('should handle async calls correctly', (done) => {
    asyncFunction().then((result) => {
        expect(result).to.equal(expectedValue);
        done();
    }).catch(done);
});
```

Mocha and Chai allow you to isolate and verify functionality, making it easy to spot issues within individual functions.

Integration Testing with Jest

Integration tests ensure that different parts of an application work well together. For a Node.js app that interacts with a database, integration testing typically verifies database interactions, API requests, or data flows between services.

- **Basic Jest Setup for Integration Tests**: Jest is highly versatile for integration testing, with built-in support for async code and mock functions.

```
const request = require('supertest');
const app = require('../app'); // The Express app instance

describe('GET /api/users', () => {
    it('should return a list of users', async () => {
        const response = await request(app).get('/api/users');
        expect(response.statusCode).toBe(200);
        expect(response.body).toHaveProperty('users');
    });
});
```

- **Mocking External Services**: If your integration tests rely on external services (like an API), use Jest's mocking functions to simulate these services and avoid dependencies in your tests.

```
jest.mock('../services/externalService');
```

Integration tests validate that your application functions correctly in a realistic environment, covering more ground than unit tests.

End-to-End Testing for Node.js Applications

End-to-end testing ensures that the application works from the user's perspective. Tools like Cypress or Jest can help automate these tests, allowing you to verify complete user flows.

- **Setting Up Cypress for E2E Testing**: Cypress is a popular tool for front-end E2E testing but works well with full-stack applications too.

```
npm install cypress --save-dev
```

- **Example E2E Test**: Write a test that simulates user actions, such as logging in, navigating pages, or submitting forms.

```
describe('User Login Flow', () => {
    it('should log in a user and redirect to dashboard', () => {
        cy.visit('/login');
        cy.get('input[name="username"]').type('user123');
        cy.get('input[name="password"]').type('password');
        cy.get('button[type="submit"]').click();
        cy.url().should('include', '/dashboard');
    });
});
```

E2E testing ensures that your application functions as expected across the full workflow, capturing issues that may not be visible in unit or integration tests.

Debugging Techniques and Best Practices

When things go wrong, debugging helps you identify the root cause and fix issues. Node.js offers various debugging tools and practices:

- **Console Logging**: Console logging is the simplest way to debug. While effective, avoid excessive use in production. Use console statements to track variable values, control flow, and errors during development.
- **Node.js Debugger**: The built-in debugger allows you to inspect and control code execution. Run your app in debug mode with:

```
node inspect app.js
```

- **Chrome DevTools**: You can debug Node.js applications using Chrome DevTools by adding the —inspect flag. This provides a graphical interface for setting breakpoints, stepping through code, and watching variables.

```
node --inspect app.js
```

- **Error Handling in Asynchronous Code**: Debugging asynchronous functions requires extra care. Use try-catch blocks with async/await and handle promise rejections to avoid unhandled exceptions.
- **Using Linting Tools**: Linters like ESLint help catch potential errors by enforcing coding standards. Run linting regularly to identify syntax errors or code patterns that may lead to issues.

```
npx eslint .
```

Proper debugging practices streamline development and reduce the time spent identifying and fixing issues.

Project: Writing Tests for the Blogging Platform API

In this project, we'll write tests for a blogging platform API to validate its functionality across different areas.

Steps:

- **Unit Tests**:
- Write unit tests for key functions such as createPost, updatePost, and deletePost. Each function should have tests for expected outcomes and error handling.
- **Integration Tests**:
- Test endpoints for creating, retrieving, updating, and deleting posts to confirm database interactions and endpoint functionality.

- Mock external dependencies, such as third-party services, to keep tests reliable.
- **End-to-End Tests**:
- Simulate a complete user flow: logging in, creating a post, updating it, and deleting it.
- Ensure user permissions are respected in these actions (e.g., only the author can delete their post).
- **Automate Tests**:
- Use a CI/CD tool to automate test execution on every pull request or push to the main branch.

By thoroughly testing the blogging platform API, we can ensure it's stable, secure, and ready for production.

Best Practices for Testing and Debugging

- **Test Coverage**: Aim for high test coverage, especially for critical components, but balance it to avoid unnecessary or redundant tests.
- **Automated Testing**: Set up a CI/CD pipeline to run tests automatically with every code change, preventing regressions.
- **Readable Error Messages**: Use descriptive error messages in tests to make it easier to understand why they failed.
- **Avoid "Flaky" Tests**: Ensure tests are stable and produce consistent results, especially E2E tests. Unreliable tests can lead to false negatives and erode confidence in the codebase.
- **Debugging with Logs**: Use structured logging libraries (like Winston or Pino) to log messages and errors in production. This makes it easier to trace issues without affecting performance.

Performance Optimization and Scalability in Node.js Applications

Memory Management in Node.js
Efficient memory usage is fundamental for high-performing applications. Memory leaks or excessive memory consumption can slow down your app, cause crashes, or lead to costly server usage. Understanding Node.js's memory model and garbage collection is a key starting point for managing memory.

- **Garbage Collection**: Node.js uses V8's garbage collector to manage memory. It automatically deallocates memory when objects are no longer in use, freeing resources. However, the garbage collector can be triggered too often if your application creates a lot of temporary objects, causing "garbage collection pauses" and reducing performance.
- **Avoiding Memory Leaks**: Common sources of memory leaks include:
- Global Variables: These persist in memory for the lifetime of the application.
- Event Listeners: Unmanaged listeners can stay active, holding references and preventing garbage collection.
- Closures: Functions with closures that reference variables from their scope can retain memory if not handled carefully.
- **Monitoring Memory Usage**: Use tools like process.memoryUsage() to monitor memory consumption and catch leaks early:

```
console.log(process.memoryUsage());
```

- **Heap Snapshots and Profiling**: Tools like Chrome DevTools can help take heap snapshots and identify objects in memory. By taking snapshots at different points, you can find which objects consume the most memory and understand potential leaks.

Event Loop Optimization: Avoiding Blocking Code

Node.js operates on a single-threaded event loop, which allows it to handle many requests concurrently. However, blocking the event loop with CPU-intensive tasks can cause delays, leading to poor performance and a sluggish user experience.

- **Identify Blocking Code**: Long-running synchronous tasks (like intensive computations) block the event loop. To identify blocking code, you can use tools like Node's —trace-sync-io flag, which traces synchronous calls and helps locate bottlenecks.
- **Offload Intensive Tasks to Worker Threads**: For CPU-bound tasks, use Worker Threads to run tasks in separate threads, keeping the main event loop free.

```
const { Worker } = require('worker_threads');
const worker = new Worker('./heavyTask.js');
```

- **Use Asynchronous Code**: Node.js thrives with non-blocking, asynchronous code. Convert blocking functions to asynchronous ones whenever possible, especially for I/O-bound tasks like database access or network requests.

Load Balancing and Scaling with Cluster Module and PM2

Node.js applications can scale horizontally, meaning multiple instances of the app can run simultaneously to handle more requests. Clustering and process management tools distribute traffic across these instances.

- **Clustering with the Node.js Cluster Module**: The cluster module allows you to create multiple instances of your app to run on different cores of a multi-core system.

```
const cluster = require('cluster');
const os = require('os');

if (cluster.isMaster) {
    const cpuCount = os.cpus().length;
    for (let i = 0; i < cpuCount; i++) {
        cluster.fork();
    }
} else {
    // Worker processes run here
    app.listen(3000);
}
```

- **Using PM2 for Process Management**: PM2 is a process manager that simplifies the clustering and scaling of Node.js apps. It also provides monitoring, log management, and automatic restarts for improved reliability.

```
pm2 start app.js -i max
```

- **Load Balancing**: A load balancer distributes incoming requests across multiple app instances, reducing the load on each and improving response times. Services like NGINX can act as a load balancer for Node.js applications:

```
upstream myapp {
    server localhost:3000;
    server localhost:3001;
}
```

Caching Strategies for Faster Responses

Caching stores frequently accessed data, reducing database queries and response times. Effective caching can lead to significant performance gains.

- **In-Memory Caching with Redis**: Redis is a popular in-memory caching tool that speeds up data retrieval. It's ideal for storing session data, query results, and other frequently requested data.

```
const redis = require('redis');
const client = redis.createClient();

client.set('key', 'value');
client.get('key', (err, result) => console.log(result));
```

- **HTTP Caching with ETags**: HTTP caching allows browsers to cache responses. ETags (entity tags) are unique identifiers for responses, allowing clients to only request resources if they've changed.

```
app.use((req, res, next) => {
    res.set('ETag', 'unique-id');
    next();
});
```

- **Content Delivery Networks (CDNs)**: CDNs cache static assets like images, CSS, and JavaScript across a network of servers, reducing load times by serving content from servers close to users.

Database Optimization Techniques

Databases are often the bottleneck in large applications. Optimizing queries and implementing caching can improve database performance.

- **Indexing**: Indexes speed up data retrieval by creating a structure for specific columns in a database. Adding indexes to frequently queried fields (like user IDs) can dramatically increase performance, especially for large tables.
- **Query Optimization**: Optimize queries to limit the amount of data retrieved. For example, using LIMIT clauses in SQL or projection in MongoDB to only retrieve necessary fields reduces load:

```
User.find({}, 'name email'); // Only retrieve name and email fields
```

- **Database Sharding**: Sharding splits large databases into smaller parts (shards), distributed across multiple servers. This allows horizontal scaling and reduces the load on individual database nodes, improving performance.

Monitoring and Profiling Tools for Node.js Performance

Ongoing monitoring is essential for identifying bottlenecks, tracking usage patterns, and ensuring that performance doesn't degrade over time.

- **Using Node.js Built-In Profiler**: Node.js provides a built-in profiler for identifying bottlenecks. You can enable profiling with:

```
node --prof app.js
```

- **Third-Party Monitoring Tools**: Tools like New Relic, Datadog, and Dynatrace offer real-time performance monitoring, helping you visualize resource usage, identify slow routes, and track memory leaks.
- **Log-Based Monitoring with Winston or Pino**: Use logging libraries to record and track errors, response times, and unusual behavior. Structured logs provide valuable insights and can be analyzed for patterns:

```
const logger = require('pino')();
logger.info('This is a log message');
```

Project: Optimizing a Data-Heavy Application for High Performance
In this project, we'll optimize a Node.js application that handles a large dataset, applying the techniques discussed to improve its performance.
Steps:

- **Identify Bottlenecks**:
- Use logging and profiling to identify areas of high CPU or memory usage. Focus on functions that handle large data or CPU-intensive tasks.
- **Optimize Database Queries**:
- Apply indexing and query optimization to reduce database query time, limiting the data retrieved and indexing key columns.
- **Implement Caching**:
- Cache frequently accessed data in Redis, especially for routes with high read-to-write ratios.
- **Use Worker Threads for CPU-Intensive Tasks**:
- Offload intensive calculations (such as data processing or analytics) to Worker Threads, keeping the main event loop free.
- **Monitor Performance in Real-Time**:

- Use a monitoring tool like Datadog to watch metrics like memory usage, response times, and request load.

Through this project, you'll gain hands-on experience with performance optimization, allowing your application to handle larger workloads and deliver faster responses.

Best Practices for Scaling and Optimizing Performance

- **Set Baselines and Track Performance**: Establish performance benchmarks and track them over time to gauge improvements or identify regressions.
- **Automate Tests for High Loads**: Use stress-testing tools like Apache JMeter or Artillery to simulate high loads and assess your app's scalability.
- **Optimize Only Where Needed**: Focus on optimizing code or areas with measurable impact on performance rather than prematurely optimizing code that doesn't affect the user experience.
- **Document Your Optimization Efforts**: Document the changes you make for performance reasons, allowing others to understand why certain code is optimized and avoiding unnecessary changes in the future.

Building Reusable Components with Microservices

Introduction to Microservices Architecture

Microservices architecture divides an application into small, autonomous services, each handling a specific function (e.g., user management, inventory, payment processing). These services are loosely coupled and can communicate through protocols such as HTTP or messaging queues. Here's why microservices are increasingly popular:

- **Independent Deployment**: Each microservice can be developed and deployed independently, which means updates or fixes can be made to a service without affecting others.
- **Scalability**: Individual services can scale separately based on demand, optimizing resources and reducing costs.
- **Fault Isolation**: If a single service fails, it doesn't necessarily bring down the entire application. This isolation helps maintain higher overall availability.

Microservices bring flexibility and resilience but also introduce complexity, requiring careful planning around communication, data management, and service orchestration.

Structuring Microservices with Node.js and Express

In a microservices-based application, each service is treated as an independent project, often with its own database, API, and business logic. Here's a typical setup:

- **Define Core Services**: Identify the main services in your application. For an e-commerce app, services might include:
- User Service: Manages user registration, login, and profile management.
- Product Service: Handles product catalog, inventory, and product details.
- Order Service: Processes orders, tracks status, and manages payment.
- Notification Service: Sends email or SMS notifications to users.
- **Organize Each Service in Separate Repositories**: Each service should have its own codebase, which helps with independent development and version control.
- **Standardize Service Structure**: Each service should have a consistent folder structure, such as:

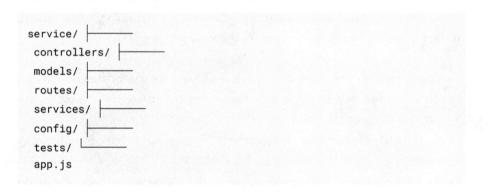

```
service/   ┝━━━━━
 controllers/  ┝━━━━━━
 models/  ┝━━━━━
 routes/  ┝━━━━━
 services/  ┝━━━━━━
 config/  ┝━━━━━
 tests/   └━━━━━
 app.js
```

- **Expose APIs for Communication**: Each service should expose an API to handle requests. Use RESTful principles to design endpoints, with clear, consistent routes and response formats.

Communication Between Microservices: HTTP, WebSocket, and Message Queues

Microservices need to communicate effectively, whether to pass data, synchronize events, or trigger actions in other services. Here are three common communication methods:

- **HTTP/REST API**:
- HTTP is the simplest and most common communication method. Services make HTTP requests to each other to share data or perform actions.
- Example: The Order Service might make an HTTP request to the Product Service to check inventory before processing an order.
- **WebSocket for Real-Time Communication**:
- For applications needing real-time updates (e.g., notifications, live chat), WebSocket enables bi-directional communication, pushing updates instantly.
- Example: The Notification Service can use WebSocket to send updates to the front-end when an order status changes.
- **Message Queues (e.g., RabbitMQ, Apache Kafka)**:
- Message queues decouple services, allowing them to send and receive messages asynchronously. This setup is ideal for tasks that don't need immediate responses, such as logging or notifications.
- Example: When an order is placed, the Order Service sends a message to the Notification Service to trigger a confirmation email.

By combining these communication methods based on specific requirements, microservices can stay loosely coupled while maintaining smooth interaction.

Managing Microservices with Docker and Kubernetes

Docker and Kubernetes are tools that simplify the deployment and management of microservices. Docker creates lightweight containers to package each service with its dependencies, and Kubernetes manages these containers at scale.

- **Containerizing Services with Docker**:
- Create a Dockerfile in each service's directory to define its runtime environment.

- Example of a Dockerfile:

```
FROM node:14
WORKDIR /app
COPY package*.json ./
RUN npm install
COPY . .
EXPOSE 3000
CMD ["npm", "start"]
```

- **Orchestrating Containers with Kubernetes**:
- Kubernetes helps manage and scale containers, automatically restarting failed services and balancing the load across containers.
- Define each service as a Kubernetes **Deployment** and expose them using **Services** within Kubernetes.
- Example of a basic deployment YAML file for a User Service:

```
apiVersion: apps/v1
kind: Deployment
metadata:
  name: user-service
spec:
  replicas: 3
  selector:
    matchLabels:
      app: user-service
  template:
    metadata:
      labels:
        app: user-service
    spec:
      containers:
      - name: user-container
```

```
image: user-service-image
ports:
- containerPort: 3000
```

Docker and Kubernetes provide a reliable, scalable infrastructure for deploying and managing microservices in production.

Project: Building a Microservices-Based E-commerce Application

To apply the concepts, we'll create an e-commerce application with separate services for users, products, and orders. Each service will run independently, communicate via HTTP and message queues, and be deployed using Docker.

Steps:

- **Set Up the User Service**:
- Build a service to manage user data (registration, login, profile updates).
- Use a database (e.g., MongoDB) to store user information.
- Expose RESTful endpoints for user-related actions.
- **Create the Product Service**:
- Manage product data, including categories, inventory, and pricing.
- Implement endpoints for creating, updating, and deleting products, as well as retrieving product information.
- Add a caching layer (e.g., Redis) to handle frequent product catalog requests efficiently.
- **Implement the Order Service**:
- Handle order placement, payment processing, and order status.
- Use HTTP requests to interact with the Product Service (for inventory checks) and the User Service (for user information).
- Send messages to the Notification Service to inform users of order updates.
- **Build the Notification Service**:
- Listen for events from other services, such as order confirmations or shipment updates.
- Use WebSocket to notify users in real-time or email to send order receipts

79

and notifications.
- **Communication and Testing**:
- Test inter-service communication with mock requests.
- Ensure that each service performs its tasks independently and only interacts with other services when needed.

By the end of this project, you'll have a functional microservices-based application with reusable services that interact effectively, demonstrating the power and flexibility of a microservices architecture.

Best Practices for Developing with Microservices

- **Decouple Services Completely**: Aim for minimal dependencies between services. Each service should be capable of running independently, reducing the risk of cascading failures.
- **Use a Centralized Logging System**: Aggregating logs from all services in a centralized platform (such as ELK Stack or Loggly) helps monitor the overall health of the application and troubleshoot issues.
- **Automate Testing and Deployment**: Ensure that each service has automated tests for functionality and deploy updates to production environments via CI/CD pipelines to reduce errors and downtime.
- **Optimize Database Design**: Each service often benefits from its own database to prevent cross-service dependencies. Choose database types based on service needs (e.g., relational databases for transactions, NoSQL for flexible data).
- **Document APIs Thoroughly**: Provide clear documentation for each service's API, making it easier for teams to understand endpoints, expected inputs/outputs, and error responses.

DevOps for Full-Stack Developers – Deployment and CI/CD

Introduction to DevOps and the Software Development Lifecycle
DevOps improves collaboration between development and operations, promoting a faster, more efficient development lifecycle. Here's how DevOps enhances each stage of the Software Development Lifecycle (SDLC):

- **Development and Integration**: With CI/CD, code is integrated frequently, enabling early detection of issues and ensuring code changes don't introduce new bugs.
- **Testing and Quality Assurance**: Automated tests run every time code is integrated, ensuring that changes meet quality standards.
- **Deployment and Delivery**: With CI/CD, applications are deployed to production more quickly and reliably, reducing downtime and manual errors.
- **Monitoring and Optimization**: DevOps promotes continuous monitoring, which helps teams track performance and catch issues early, providing a more stable experience for users.

By adopting DevOps, development teams can deliver more features, respond to feedback faster, and improve system reliability.

Setting Up a CI/CD Pipeline with GitHub Actions and Jenkins

A CI/CD pipeline automates the steps involved in building, testing, and deploying applications. Popular CI/CD tools include **GitHub Actions** (integrated with GitHub) and **Jenkins** (an open-source automation server). Here's a quick overview of each:

- **GitHub Actions**: GitHub Actions offers an easy-to-configure environment for CI/CD, especially for projects hosted on GitHub. Each "workflow" defines steps for building, testing, and deploying.

Example Workflow: Create a .github/workflows/ci.yml file to define the CI/CD pipeline.

```
name: CI/CD Pipeline
on:
  push:
    branches:
      - main
jobs:
  build:
    runs-on: ubuntu-latest
    steps:
      - name: Checkout Code
        uses: actions/checkout@v2

      - name: Set up Node.js
        uses: actions/setup-node@v2
        with:
          node-version: '14'

      - name: Install Dependencies
        run: npm install

      - name: Run Tests
        run: npm test

      - name: Deploy to Production
        if: github.ref == 'refs/heads/main'
```

```
run: ./deploy.sh
```

In this workflow, the steps include checking out the code, setting up Node.js, installing dependencies, running tests, and deploying to production if changes are pushed to the main branch.

- **Jenkins**: Jenkins is a more flexible option for CI/CD, capable of integrating with a variety of version control systems. It runs jobs (or builds) that can execute scripts for building, testing, and deploying code.
- Basic Jenkins Setup:
- Create a Jenkins job, select "Pipeline," and define the pipeline script.
- Example:

```
pipeline {
    agent any
    stages {
        stage('Install Dependencies') {
            steps {
                sh 'npm install'
            }
        }
        stage('Run Tests') {
            steps {
                sh 'npm test'
            }
        }
        stage('Deploy') {
            when {
                branch 'main'
            }
            steps {
                sh './deploy.sh'
            }
        }
    }
}
```

Both tools allow developers to automate repetitive tasks, minimize manual interventions, and maintain consistent workflows.

Containerization with Docker: Creating Docker Images for Node.js Apps

Containerization packages an application and its dependencies into a single unit called a container. Docker is a popular tool for containerization, ensuring consistency across different environments.

- **Creating a Dockerfile**: A Dockerfile specifies how to build the Docker image for your application. Here's an example for a Node.js app:

```
# Use the official Node.js image
FROM node:14

# Set the working directory
WORKDIR /app

# Copy package files and install dependencies
COPY package*.json ./
RUN npm install

# Copy application code
COPY . .

# Expose port and define the start command
EXPOSE 3000
CMD ["npm", "start"]
```

- **Building and Running the Docker Image**:
- Build the Docker image:

```
docker build -t my-node-app .
```

- Run the Docker container:

```
docker run -p 3000:3000 my-node-app
```

- **Using Docker Compose for Multi-Container Applications**: For applications with multiple services (e.g., a Node.js app with a MongoDB database), Docker Compose can orchestrate these containers. Define a docker-compose.yml file:

```
version: '3'
services:
  app:
    build: .
    ports:
      - "3000:3000"
  db:
    image: mongo
    ports:
      - "27017:27017"
```

Docker standardizes the application environment, making it easier to deploy and manage applications in production.

Cloud Deployment Options: AWS, Heroku, DigitalOcean

Deploying applications to the cloud allows for scalability, reliability, and easy management. Here's a look at deploying Node.js apps on three popular platforms:

- **AWS (Amazon Web Services)**: AWS offers various services for deployment, including EC2 (Elastic Compute Cloud), Elastic Beanstalk, and Lambda.

- Elastic Beanstalk: Simplifies deployment by managing the infrastructure, scaling, and environment setup. Upload the application, and Elastic Beanstalk handles the rest.
- AWS Lambda: For serverless applications, Lambda allows running code without managing servers. Ideal for microservices or event-driven tasks.
- **Heroku**: Heroku is a platform-as-a-service (PaaS) with a straightforward deployment process, making it a good choice for smaller applications or MVPs. It manages servers, scaling, and monitoring for you.
- Deploying to Heroku:

```
heroku create my-node-app
git push heroku main
```

- **DigitalOcean**: DigitalOcean offers Droplets (virtual machines) and App Platform (a fully managed platform). App Platform automates deployment, scaling, and management.

Each platform has its unique features, pricing, and performance. Choose based on the project's scale, budget, and expected traffic.

Project: Deploying a Full-Stack Application to AWS Using Docker and CI/CD

In this project, we'll deploy a full-stack Node.js application to AWS, using Docker for containerization and GitHub Actions for CI/CD.

Steps:

- **Set Up Docker for the Application**:
- Create a Dockerfile and Docker Compose configuration if the application has multiple services.

- **Push the Docker Image to Amazon ECR (Elastic Container Registry)**:
- Amazon ECR stores container images, making them available for deployment across AWS services.

```
aws ecr create-repository --repository-name my-app
docker tag my-app:latest
<your-account-id>.dkr.ecr.<region>.amazonaws.com/my-app:latest
docker push
<your-account-id>.dkr.ecr.<region>.amazonaws.com/my-app:latest
```

- **Deploy to AWS Elastic Beanstalk**:
- Use the Elastic Beanstalk CLI to deploy your Docker container to Elastic Beanstalk.

```
eb init -p docker my-app
eb create my-app-env
```

- **Set Up a CI/CD Workflow with GitHub Actions**:
- Define a GitHub Actions workflow to automate testing and deployment on each code push to the main branch.

By completing this project, you'll understand how to containerize, deploy, and automate a Node.js application on AWS, achieving a streamlined CI/CD process.

Best Practices for DevOps in Full-Stack Development

- **Automate Where Possible**: Use CI/CD to automate repetitive tasks, reducing manual errors and ensuring consistency in your deployment process.

- **Monitor Application Health**: Use monitoring tools (e.g., AWS Cloud-Watch, New Relic) to track resource usage, uptime, and performance. Monitoring helps detect issues early and optimize application performance.

- **Secure Secrets and Configurations**: Store sensitive data (e.g., API keys, credentials) in environment variables or secret managers (e.g., AWS Secrets Manager) to protect against unauthorized access.

- **Document Your DevOps Processes**: Clear documentation ensures your team understands the CI/CD pipeline, deployment processes, and troubleshooting steps, making collaboration more effective.

- **Rollbacks and Versioning**: Ensure the ability to roll back deployments in case of failure. Use versioned releases or tags to keep track of stable versions, and implement automated rollback strategies where possible.

Real-World Case Studies and Best Practices

C ase Study 1: Building a Scalable Social Media App
Creating a social media application requires handling large volumes of user data, images, and real-time interactions. This example covers the design and implementation of a scalable social media app with features like user posts, comments, notifications, and messaging.

Key Elements:

- **Architecture**: Microservices structure to separate services for users, posts, notifications, and messaging.
- **Real-Time Functionality**: WebSockets and message queues (e.g., RabbitMQ) for real-time notifications and messaging.
- **Database Choices**: Use of a NoSQL database (like MongoDB) for user-generated content and a SQL database for transactions requiring consistency.

Best Practices Implemented:

- **Horizontal Scaling**: Set up load balancers to distribute traffic across instances, ensuring the app can handle increased user loads.
- **Content Delivery Network (CDN)**: Cached static content (e.g., images, CSS) through a CDN to reduce server load and improve response times.
- **Rate Limiting and Throttling**: Implemented rate limiting to manage

API request loads and protect against potential abuse.

Challenges and Solutions:

- **Challenge**: Handling real-time updates without slowing down the app.
- **Solution**: Used WebSockets for instant messaging and notifications, while batching updates for lower-priority notifications.

Through this example, we see how scalability and real-time interactivity can coexist in an application designed to support millions of users.

Case Study 2: Creating a Real-Time Data Dashboard with WebSockets
A real-time data dashboard provides live updates, such as sales data, user activity, or market data, which requires low-latency data handling. This case study explores how a real-time dashboard was implemented to monitor user interactions and sales data.

Key Elements:

- **Backend**: Node.js and Express framework for API and WebSocket handling.
- **Frontend**: React and D3.js for dynamic data visualization, allowing data updates to render seamlessly in real-time.
- **Data Management**: In-memory caching for high-speed data access, with Redis storing frequently accessed data to reduce response times.

Best Practices Implemented:

- **WebSocket Integration**: WebSocket connections push updates directly to the client whenever data changes, ensuring immediate visibility for users.
- **Data Throttling**: Limited data updates to avoid overwhelming the front-end with high-frequency updates, keeping data display manageable and relevant.

- **Efficient Data Visualization**: D3.js enabled the dashboard to render graphs and tables with minimal lag, improving the user experience.

Challenges and Solutions:

- **Challenge**: Ensuring real-time accuracy while managing server resources.
- **Solution**: Used Redis as a buffer to manage data flow, ensuring that the app didn't overuse memory while handling frequent data updates.

This case study demonstrates how to use WebSockets and caching to build a responsive data dashboard that provides real-time insights without sacrificing performance.

Case Study 3: Developing a Secure Financial Transactions API

Building an API for financial transactions introduces specific requirements around security, data integrity, and high availability. This example highlights the development of a secure transaction API for a payment gateway.

Key Elements:

- **Authentication and Authorization**: Implemented JWT for user authentication and role-based access control (RBAC) for restricted functions.
- **Database**: SQL database with ACID compliance to ensure transaction integrity and reliability.
- **Encryption**: Used SSL/TLS for secure data transmission and bcrypt for password hashing.

Best Practices Implemented:

- **Data Encryption**: All sensitive data was encrypted both in transit and at rest, ensuring that data is protected even if intercepted.
- **Input Validation and Sanitization**: Validated all user inputs to prevent SQL injection and other potential attacks.

- **Detailed Audit Logs**: Recorded all transactions and changes to provide an audit trail, allowing for tracking in case of security incidents.

Challenges and Solutions:

- **Challenge**: Maintaining performance with multiple security layers.
- **Solution**: Used optimized queries and database indexing to keep response times low despite the high-security requirements.

This case study underscores the importance of security best practices in protecting sensitive financial data and maintaining user trust.

Lessons Learned: Best Practices and Common Pitfalls in Full-Stack Development

Building successful full-stack applications requires balancing performance, security, and scalability while also keeping the development process efficient. Here are some critical lessons from the case studies and general industry best practices.

Best Practices:

- **Modular Architecture**: Break down applications into manageable components or services. Whether using microservices or modular components within a monolithic structure, this approach makes it easier to test, debug, and scale parts of the application independently.
- **Efficient Use of Caching**: Caching (both client-side and server-side) reduces database load and response times. Use tools like Redis for server caching and ETags for HTTP caching to improve performance.
- **Thorough Testing Strategy**: Cover all testing stages—unit, integration, and end-to-end testing. Automated testing ensures code quality and reduces errors before deployment.
- **Error Handling and Logging**: Implement robust error handling and centralized logging to monitor application health. Tools like Winston or Pino for logging and monitoring services like New Relic or Datadog help

detect issues early.

- **Secure Coding Practices**: Always follow secure coding practices, such as using HTTPS, hashing passwords, validating user inputs, and setting up secure environment variables.

Common Pitfalls:

- **Ignoring Scalability Early**: Designing without considering scalability can lead to bottlenecks and costly refactoring later. Adopt scalable design patterns, even in early stages, for smoother growth.
- **Skipping Documentation**: Well-documented code and APIs make it easier for new developers to understand the application and ensure consistency, especially in a team setting.
- **Overlooking Optimization**: Premature optimization can complicate code unnecessarily. Instead, measure performance, identify real bottlenecks, and optimize where there's clear evidence of performance issues.
- **Neglecting DevOps Integration**: CI/CD and DevOps practices streamline testing and deployment, reducing human error. Without it, manual deployment can become error-prone and time-consuming.

Bonus Project: Implementing Best Practices in an Enterprise-Grade Application

This project aims to apply the best practices discussed in building an enterprise-grade application. We'll create a robust API for a service-based application, focusing on scalability, security, performance, and reliability.

Steps:

- **Define Requirements and Architecture**:
- Identify the core services, such as user management, billing, and notifications.
- Use microservices architecture for scalability, with each service running independently.
- **Implement Authentication and Authorization**:

- Use JWT for stateless authentication.
- Set up role-based access control for different levels of permissions.
- **Integrate Caching and Load Balancing**:
- Implement server-side caching with Redis to reduce load on the database.
- Use NGINX or a cloud-based load balancer to distribute traffic across multiple instances.
- **Set Up CI/CD Pipeline**:
- Automate testing and deployment with GitHub Actions or Jenkins.
- Configure the pipeline to run tests on each commit and deploy automatically to a staging environment before production.
- **Deploy and Monitor**:
- Deploy the application to a cloud platform (AWS, GCP, or Azure) using Docker and Kubernetes.
- Use monitoring tools (e.g., CloudWatch, New Relic) to track performance, set up alerts for errors, and maintain high availability.

Through this bonus project, you'll apply best practices across the development lifecycle, creating a reliable, scalable, and maintainable application.

Additional Tools and Resources for Full-Stack Developers

1. Development and Code Editing Tools

A powerful code editor or Integrated Development Environment (IDE) forms the foundation of any development workflow. Here are some of the most popular editors for full-stack developers:

- **Visual Studio Code (VS Code)**: VS Code is widely regarded for its flexibility, with an extensive marketplace for extensions. Essential plugins for full-stack development include:
- **Prettier** for code formatting
- **ESLint** for linting JavaScript and TypeScript
- **Debugger for Chrome** for debugging frontend code
- **REST Client** for testing APIs directly in the editor
- **WebStorm**: Known for robust support for JavaScript frameworks, WebStorm is popular among full-stack developers who work with React, Angular, or Vue.
- **Atom**: Another lightweight editor, Atom, offers flexibility and integrates well with GitHub. While less common now, it remains a choice for some developers looking for simple and customizable tools.

2. Version Control and Collaboration

Efficient collaboration is essential in modern development, especially when working in teams. These tools improve collaboration, version tracking, and workflow management:

- **Git and GitHub**: GitHub hosts code repositories and facilitates collaboration through pull requests, code reviews, and discussions. GitHub Actions is an added feature that allows you to set up CI/CD workflows.
- **GitLab**: GitLab combines Git repository management with CI/CD, making it a comprehensive platform for code hosting, CI/CD, and DevOps integration.
- **Bitbucket**: Another Git repository hosting service, Bitbucket integrates well with Jira and Trello, making it ideal for teams already using these Atlassian tools.

3. Debugging and Testing Tools

Debugging and testing are crucial for identifying and resolving issues before production. Here are some tools that make this process easier:

- **Postman**: Postman simplifies API testing by allowing developers to send HTTP requests and inspect responses. It's ideal for verifying backend endpoints and API interactions.
- **Mocha and Chai**: Mocha is a popular test framework for Node.js, and Chai provides assertion functions, making it easier to verify test results.
- **Jest**: Jest is a testing framework popular with JavaScript developers, especially for React applications. It supports unit testing, integration testing, and mocking.
- **Cypress**: Cypress is an end-to-end testing tool ideal for web applications. Its interactive nature makes it easy to track the entire testing process visually, ensuring everything works as expected from a user's perspective.
- **Sentry**: Sentry is an error-tracking tool that monitors applications for crashes, uncaught exceptions, and performance issues, allowing developers to catch bugs before they impact users.

4. Frontend Libraries and Frameworks

Frontend frameworks and libraries simplify user interface creation, al-

96

lowing developers to focus on building features instead of handling basic functionalities.

- **React**: React is a component-based library for building UIs, particularly popular for single-page applications (SPAs). The React ecosystem includes libraries for state management (like Redux) and routing (React Router).
- **Vue.js**: Vue is a flexible, progressive JavaScript framework with a simple API. It's user-friendly for beginners and offers robust features like Vuex for state management and Vue Router.
- **Angular**: Angular is a comprehensive framework backed by Google, offering built-in tools for routing, state management, and form handling. It's a solid choice for large, enterprise-grade applications.

5. Backend Libraries and Frameworks

The backend of an application manages business logic, data storage, and security. Here are key libraries and frameworks for Node.js developers:

- **Express.js**: A minimalist web framework for Node.js, Express simplifies server creation and routing. Its middleware architecture allows developers to extend its capabilities with libraries for authentication, logging, and more.
- **NestJS**: NestJS is a framework for building scalable server-side applications, particularly popular for complex, enterprise-level applications. It uses TypeScript and encourages modular code organization.
- **Socket.io**: For real-time communication, such as chat applications, Socket.io provides an easy way to implement WebSocket functionality, enabling instant data transfer between client and server.
- **Mongoose**: Mongoose is an Object Data Modeling (ODM) library for MongoDB and Node.js, making it easier to work with MongoDB databases by defining schemas, validation, and query-building functions.

6. Database Management and Querying

A strong understanding of databases and data management tools is essential for full-stack development. Here are popular database tools and libraries:

- **MongoDB**: A NoSQL database that stores data in JSON-like documents, MongoDB is often paired with Node.js. MongoDB Atlas provides managed hosting for deploying MongoDB clusters.
- **PostgreSQL**: A powerful relational database, PostgreSQL is known for its stability and support for complex queries, making it a good choice for data-intensive applications.
- **Sequelize**: Sequelize is an ORM (Object-Relational Mapper) for SQL databases, offering a robust querying syntax and the ability to interact with databases like PostgreSQL, MySQL, and SQLite.
- **Redis**: Redis is an in-memory database often used for caching, which can improve performance by storing frequently accessed data.

7. Deployment and DevOps Tools

Deployment and DevOps tools allow developers to streamline the release process, ensuring applications run smoothly and efficiently.

- **Docker**: Docker containerizes applications, bundling them with their dependencies, making deployment and scaling much easier. Docker Compose simplifies multi-container applications.
- **Kubernetes**: Kubernetes is a container orchestration tool that manages, scales, and automates containerized applications, ideal for large-scale applications with multiple services.
- **Heroku**: Heroku is a Platform-as-a-Service (PaaS) that simplifies deployment by handling infrastructure, making it a good choice for small to medium-sized applications.
- **AWS and Google Cloud Platform (GCP)**: Both platforms provide comprehensive cloud services, from storage to compute power, with options for deploying containerized applications, serverless functions, and managed databases.
- **Jenkins**: Jenkins is a popular CI/CD tool that automates building,

testing, and deploying code, supporting integration with various code repositories and deployment platforms.

8. Monitoring and Logging

Keeping track of application health and performance is essential to identify issues early and maintain reliability.

- **New Relic**: New Relic is a performance monitoring tool that provides insights into application performance, transaction times, and server health.
- **Datadog**: Datadog offers a suite of tools for monitoring infrastructure, application performance, and logs, making it suitable for complex applications.
- **Winston and Pino**: Both Winston and Pino are logging libraries for Node.js, with capabilities for custom logging levels, log rotation, and integration with external logging services.
- **ELK Stack (Elasticsearch, Logstash, Kibana)**: The ELK Stack is a set of tools for managing and visualizing logs, making it easier to identify trends, errors, and issues.

9. Recommended Resources and Further Learning Paths

Keeping your skills current is crucial in the fast-evolving tech industry. Here are some valuable resources for continuous learning:

- **MDN Web Docs**: MDN offers comprehensive documentation on web standards and JavaScript, an essential resource for frontend and full-stack developers.
- **Node.js Documentation**: The official Node.js documentation provides in-depth guides on Node's core modules, APIs, and libraries.
- **FreeCodeCamp and Codecademy**: Both platforms offer interactive courses on JavaScript, Node.js, and full-stack development, ideal for hands-on practice.
- **Egghead.io**: Egghead.io features short, practical video tutorials on

frontend and backend development topics, including frameworks like React, Vue, and Node.js.

- **Books**:
- *Eloquent JavaScript* by Marijn Haverbeke: A classic book on JavaScript, covering both frontend and backend concepts.
- *You Don't Know JS* by Kyle Simpson: An in-depth series exploring core JavaScript concepts.
- *Designing Data-Intensive Applications* by Martin Kleppmann: A deep dive into data management, storage, and processing.
- **Communities**:
- **Stack Overflow**: A valuable Q&A platform for solving technical issues.
- **Reddit** (/r/webdev, /r/node, /r/javascript): Subreddits are helpful for discussions, project ideas, and staying updated on industry trends.
- **Dev.to**: A community platform where developers share articles, tutorials, and insights.

10. GitHub Repository for Code Samples and Solutions

Maintaining a GitHub repository for personal projects, code snippets, and solved challenges is an excellent way to track your progress and share your skills. Building a portfolio of your code is valuable for job applications and collaboration.

- **Create Organized Repositories**: Structure your repositories with README files, documentation, and clear directory structures for easy navigation.
- **Contribute to Open Source Projects**: Contributing to open source projects on GitHub can improve your skills and showcase your ability to work in real-world environments.
- **Use GitHub Pages**: Host project documentation or personal websites using GitHub Pages, creating a professional online presence.